A Map in my Blood

A Map in my Blood

Carla Braidek

thistledown press

Thistledown Press Ltd.
410 2nd Avenue North
Saskatoon, Saskatchewan, S7K 2C3
www.thistledownpress.com

Library and Archives Canada Cataloguing in Publication

Braidek, Carla, 1958–, author
A map in my blood / Carla Braidek.

Poems.
ISBN 978-1-77187-096-2 (paperback)

I. Title.

PS8603.R337M36 2016 C811'.6 C2016-901044-9

Cover: fibre artwork by Rita St. Amant
Author photo by Meadow McLean
Cover and book design by Jackie Forrie
Printed and bound in Canada

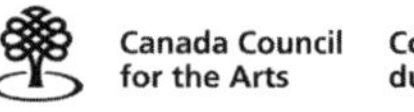

Canada

Thistledown Press gratefully acknowledges the financial assistance of the Canada Council for the Arts, the Saskatchewan Arts Board, and the Government of Canada through the Canada Book Fund for its publishing program.

Acknowledgements

Loud and energetic applause to Sans Nom writers group for their support and the wonderful retreats. Extra hugs to Lynda Monahan and Jan Wood for poetic advice, editing assistance and loving attention to this poet.

Much appreciation to Steven Ross Smith for his keen editor's eye and fine-tuned ear.

I also acknowledge the Saskatchewan Arts Board and the Saskatchewan Writers Guild for the retreats offered in the winter of every year at St. Peter's in Muenster, Saskatchewan. Time alone, and the opportunity to engage with other writers, is invaluable.

Thank you to Leaf Press, *Room*, *Antigonish Review*, *Other Voices* and *Transition* magazines for publishing previous incarnations of some of these poems. Thanks also to Hagios Press for my work being included in the anthology 'Fast Forward'.

EMMA International Artists Collaboration has my heartfelt gratitude for giving me an amazing opportunity. There is nothing like playing with like-minded people to discover how fun making can be.

Love as always to Garry. His willingness to let me wander my own world for as long as it takes does not go unnoticed.

Finally a big hug to my children and their children for all their love; it makes my difficulties fade away.

Contents

This book is for my family, near and far, who have walked pieces of this journey with me, but especially for my mom, Joan, who led by her good example and was always ready for adventure.

Where Do I Begin?

with the broken ankle
the slip on the wet ramp
how my toes went under
the bone snapped and I
threw myself back

or should I start with breakfast
toast and an orange
the new tea I found last week
at the shop in Saskatoon
the sweet scent reassuring

perhaps begin with my leaving last week
to fix Heather's deck in the distant city
coming home early to singular quiet
peace not often mine

castles dissolve in the slow
rains of summer and time
wheels around the block the way
Trish and I wove between children
and cars on our way to the park
bicycles tossed aside and sun
slanting across the field

how do we know where a moment begins?
when time draws itself down
to hunker at the edge of the sandbox
where small greedy hands reach for cars
pressed along roads created by a stick
then erased
by a careless knee or the slip
of days into years

The Day They Paved Our Street

we crouch 10 a.m. panting in the measly shade of a
tree as tall as my dad   as big as my skinny wrist
yellow trucks raise dust from our dirt-clay street
belch smoke   ooze tar
men with muscular arms have no time for kids
steaming loads of crumbly asphalt
cascade from raised boxes
while mothers watch us watch

flies climb the backs of my sticky legs
Mom pushes curls from her forehead
bubble-gum tar sends heat waves into shimmering air
men's shirts cling to their backs in dark patches
and their faces don't wipe dry with a swipe of handkerchief

Mom's voice rises as we lean over the curb
to press a precious nickel into steaming blacktop
we retreat to an uncracked front step
lie belly down on cool cement
watch rakes and blackened shovels smooth the pebbly heaps
but most amazing is the gigantic roller

tin lunch kits lie open in the shade of a truck
with no motor running   men's eyes close
we follow Mom inside to the huge white fridge
where fog rolls out and she spoons
cool scoops into crisp cones

four of us   two treats apiece
cross the new lawn where
men's eyes widen   grins stretch their brown faces
and I trade dripping white
for grease on my knuckle

Twitch

the hind leg of my dog pumps
and I believe he dreams

I'm not alone
the brother I rarely speak to kneels at my side
we lay our hands lightly on dog fur over the ribs
we want to be inside
against those smooth muscles
as they draw and stretch
elastic bands at his hips
flexing

we want whatever it is
that makes his nose twitch
don't even consider it may be
the dead gopher that greases the road
we imagine what we know
juicy bones and puppy treats
have yet to learn that guts and blood
the sweet stench of ferment
deserve our yearning

the dog sleeps hard
doesn't budge as we lift
the eyelid of his shaggy face

A Woman Walks

at eight she tumbled loose on backyard grass
flung herself into leaps and somersaults
cartwheeled over obstacles

at fourteen she trained in the gym
backbends into walkovers
always honing the edge

at twenty-five she realizes
she should have trained for the marathon
better yet the triathlon

she wonders about her ability to bend
her loss of limber
the disconcerting lack of balance

she stumbles through the week
dreams of walking on her hands

Acts of Balance

I want balance
not the physical aptitude needed
to stand on new rafters two stories up
people circling below engrossed
in tasks while relying on me
to tack down the plywood

I want the aplomb that catches me
when I teeter at the brink of my capacity
lets me dance the edge of a 2 x 4
weigh the odds and come up even enough
to pull it all together with a quick
hammer and well-placed nails

I dread the dropped knot in my stomach
when I am so very near open air
and may in fact be already plummeting
my daughter demands fairness and freedom
as I verge on shouts to make my point
my throat tightens so not to slip further

there is no blueprint to alter
no lines to erase or new marks to add
just a blank sheet crackling in this relentless
wind that leaves me dishevelled
we sway in efforts for poise
the entire arrangement teeters

balance
as shy of me as the fisher that slid away last week
when we were canoeing
the creature's dark body a sinuous shadow in the brush
our awe and satisfaction   a moment of equilibrium

A Matter of Waiting

I cut the morning into stars of apple
expose a glimmer of white within red
tumble them down into a cobalt blue
bowl next to the apricot jam

plates circle the table like tires
on the bicycle collapsed on the lawn
means to a dream of motors and dust
sunlight on spokes as the crowd roars
and you my son are the glint in everyone's eye

mugs cannot match your defiance
your determination to push the edge
they settle firmly in place while you
careen around corners
sail over rough edges at a mere
glimpse of stars winking in a bowl

I let you choose the one you want
every second there's another as I slice and stars
fall across the table   I remember
it's all a matter of waiting
    while the tree grows roots then branches
    flowers open and the bee comes
waiting while the fruit thickens
patiently   patiently
until it says pick me
and I do

Heart's Breath

at the powwow my granddaughter bounces against my leg
moves her tiny moccasins in time with the big drum
she grins as her head bobs

for nine months she lay curled in dark
her mother's drum the beat she moved with

now this circle
spins on tradition
swirls of shawls
feathers abustle
jingles clash beneath the sun
beads flash as children run
voices rise
the drum compels
feet to step
        and step

hearts pulse   earth throbs
we breathe   she bobs

To Find a Way

I cannot put a finger on my discomfort
but it's like walking into nettles
a pattern of welts on my skin
the irritating reminder of having lost my way
I wait anxiously for some innate sense of north to kick in
remember   *stay in one place*
remain calm   they will find you
        no one is looking

I am lost as the tall ships that sailed into the gleam
of a dragon's unforgiving eyes at the edge of the map
perhaps I should slash the throat of a new-born calf
let the blood spray onto a blank sheet of snow
read the tracings at the height of the sun
then follow as it bids me
    or I could dig deep
unearth a crystal ball
scry its secrets and move accordingly

my grandfather's grandfather stood beneath night sky
considered constellations to plot his course
wind over fields luring him one way
a high wall of alder forcing him another
he read the stars to cross unmarred prairie
made his slow way through the densest bush
learned the land by listening to its pulse

there's a map in my blood
it cools and burns

To Dad

We work the trees, you and I — research roots, observe branches, note changes and mutations. You dig into the past, trace from parent to child to child, link cousins across time. My hands sift peat, adjust the seeder, clean the spruce seed waiting to become the next crop. Thoughtfully you choose what to include on the page; you prune words yet our story grows. You tell of a name that changes as it travels, possibly from the sands of Egypt, to the Ukraine, to Canada. You write of uncles who avoided war through suicide and disappearance. Grandpa's horses kept him safe as he was considered necessary at home. Grandma's ability in English and Ukrainian brought the old country to the new land, kept people in touch in spite of an ocean of change. They planted seeds of carrot and wheat, threw chunks of potato into new soil. I am given some tree seed, select others. As the days pass I admire the tender stems drawing their heads out of the peat. Fertilizer is chosen for rooting, another for rapid growth. I keep notes of the varied results based on the growing regime. My hands brush over the small spruce trees the way a grandmother lightly runs her hand over the head of a child dashing by. Your paperwork brings the past to life, while I try to give life to the future. The tiny seeds I sow grow into towering trees, bear their parents' traits that alter as they stretch into tomorrow's branches. You have seen tomorrow coming; have watched dreams dim to accepted reality. Your children and grandchildren bear both your potential and your disappointments. We share this tree, you and I, sun and shadow ghosting at our feet.

Speak Copper

planish
anneal

I am learning a new language

my body remembers the way copper rings in the sun
the heft of the hammer
the pinch of the vise

ball-peen
stake

select a sheet of copper
the weight is up to you
cut it with tools like scissors
alligator jaws tamed just enough they will
take your finger off if you are careless
discover the awkwardness of right angles
the impossibility of acute

crease the metal
lay the piece over a notch in the stump
begin the groove that becomes a fold
let the welding hammer blaze the trail
diligently fold the copper over itself
tap gently   make it become
something you are thinking about
give it enough space to still be itself

deliver it to the fire
heat will make it malleable
now it gives
wants to move
wants to become something else

so help it out
take the hammer and pound
carefully
with focus
this is serious

and it's not

it's *hide'n'seek*
and *run rabbit run*
but mostly it's a beginning
the shape of a mouth finding its tongue

learn burnish
file   patina   quench
speak copper

Beyond

coyotes howl across the river
there's no more wood on the landing

cattails sway in a restless wind
worms fret beneath yesterday's garden

red osiers point and weep and point
anemones ghost the lane by the bridge

rain dapples stone until appaloosa blankets
rumple on hills beyond the pasture gate

I rock in the dark   dream
every new leaf a flag on the hill

Fingers Like Wings

Gloves — not the flimsy knitted gloves that let fingers feel the wind as it moves between aspen on prairie. Nor those fine leather gloves, smooth as the day they left their box, needlework down the backs like bird-stitched tracks along the ribs of a fallow field. The fields where geese gather are not fallow. They are fields that have been worked; that are working to grow barley, oats, canola, peas.

And these gloves are working gloves — the ones left on the grass next to the newly planted poplar — four-foot whips that will stand in the wind, the way a finger hangs in the air, a marker, a question. Trees that start with a lean, unlike the fence posts that stand straight, until age or an itchy animal forces them over — the itch in the hide causes the rub and the snag of the barb rends the glove, exposes skin.

These are gloves with the thumb and first fingertip worn open from grasping staples, holding them steady for the tap/whack of the hammer — the occasional sing of wire when the hammer slips. Leather so thin fingers can read the splits and knots of each post as it's loaded then held upright, to await the heavy head of the post-pounder, much like we stand in the lull of autumn, appraise the year, anticipate the weight of winter.

All the branches free before they fill with snow, before the fields flatten with white. We brace ourselves prior to the effort of keeping the car running, the road passable. Prepare for the bother of an extra sweater and a toque, for gloves fallen from pockets. They trail on the path like bread crumbs marking, not the way back, but the place we fly forward from, fingers splayed into wind.

The Only One

Grandpa took us to the garden behind the garage
showed us how to pull peas and where strawberries hid
his peonies in the backyard
interrupted our games and races

it was Grandpa who took us to the gravel pit
brought home sand in the car trunk
carefully scooped it into the hollow under the big elm
so we could build roads and castles

Grandpa was tall enough to reach things on the top shelf
but was too tall for the stairwell to the basement
his long thin arms reached way down
to hold our young hands in his large veiny ones

Grandpa let us use his putter
down in the fixed-up basement room
we spent rainy Sunday afternoons tapping golf balls
from the couch to the soft rubber platter

when the boys were old enough Grandpa took them golfing
each summer for a weekend at Watrous
a boys' weekend for cousins and brothers
girls not welcome   even if we asked

when they came home again
my brothers wanted to play games
but they didn't always know the rules
for I am the only one
Grandpa taught to play checkers

Rules for Play

some people prefer board games
    the correct number of pieces
    two die and carefully counted money
    an optional approach if the game becomes too difficult

they are the ones who read non-fiction
    insist upon diagrams
    appreciate well-written drama based
    on history with no surprise endings

they drive state-of-the-art fuel-injected molded-fiberglass vehicles
    carry palm pilots
    and rely on surge-protected modems
    to keep them hooked up   plugged in

I like it simple
    wooden toys
        short poems
            a bicycle

Hide and Seek

delight in the tickle of feathers
the scritch of claws against palm
know the caprice of holding

a heart corralled in a bone net
flutters briefly in the throat
before the sky leans into indigo

listen as jays cry   juncos creep the damp earth
they fear your quick hand that beats the bush
for the ghost of your mother

she lingers   checking for clean underwear
preparing picnics on hillsides
ready or not here she comes

Slivers

I.

once more she pulls pliers from the toolbox
carries them onto the deck
grabs leather gloves on the way
and slips into a heavy plaid jacket
there's a miserable dog tied to a post
and a lost man waiting
how many times will this animal run
into the bush   scent down a porcupine
and be unable to resist the urge?

memory must hold quills and pliers
must be trussed by rope and bundled by blanket
there is no way even a dog's small brain
could not retain the trauma
but the sliver of desire that courses through him
when scent comes and movement in underbrush tantalizes
is more than he can tolerate
he leans into it

II.

why not leave those quills wild
or at least allow someone else to tame them
someone who would coax them into moccasins
or mittens   hide and beads with quills
brought together by patient hands
not wasted
stuck in a lower jaw
upper jaw   back of throat
this is worse than she thought

the woman takes each dream for success
every notion for change
pierces it with logic and caution that zings
like lemon juice in an open wound
the sourness festers
into a lump nothing can pass
stuck as it is in the man's throat
he cannot talk   can barely breathe
each objection is a plug that stops his world

III.

the wedge driven through heartwood
splits spruce into tatters of trees
spires shredded to flags at half-mast

all hover in hunger and sway
with the birch by the lake
that casual swirl of branches
hinged from their middles
where the moon rides
and swells
a pumpkin of an idea
with all the potential of becoming
a pie   warm and well-rounded

but who would it feed?
not the dog who lays by the step
his throat swollen with quills
not the man who sits in the chair
pliers loose in his hand
nor the woman hunkered down
halfway between man and dog
slowly working a sliver
out of her own thumb

Field Stones

more solid than the land you lifted them from
contrary to the wind that harries the grass
making it talk long after you want silence

years of lichen creep rust across boulders
cling to the curves that tumbled
as they turned beneath plow and shovel

all your youth rests in the void
that marked the edge of the meadow
it sleeps beneath a blanket of northern bedstraw
laced with sky spots of asters

bring those flowers to the house
drop them into cool water   clear in an old jar
the mark of hardness a ring around its middle
like the stain of sun that etches your hands and face

permanent

Red Willow Baskets

elder
I don't recall your name
remember instead your hands
brown with wrinkled skin and strong
the second knuckle on your right hand large with old injury
the slash across your thumb healed in a ridge

elder
who gave me baskets of beauty
your smooth voice wove words of supple wisdom
like the willows we cut carefully
you explained how to test for strength
what to select and what to reject
how to find the breaking point

you spoke of the future
the tending
how to trim the branch
just above the bud
to ensure it gave new growth
to bend about a sturdy frame

for the frame you recommended ash
straight and true
branches parting from the stem in clean duality
wood honest enough to hold
where it curves at the rim
or crooks to a handle

elder
every basket you fashion ferries your words
beyond the bend of each withy
through each arc of ash

Dream

in the warm air of summer all flows like water
small splashes the greatest disturbance to expect
consider butterflies at the edge of a puddle
the ease of soft talk in dappled shade

as heat subsides into autumn
the creep of frost is a wedge between people
colours leech from plants
a gap widens within me

tight questions of willow leaves
frost-killed on the stem
query long into winter

wind and lakeshore reeds shuffle answers
until stillness becomes a wound

cold bares her teeth
gnaws on the snowy road
as it turns and turns away

haggard days between long visits
conversations deep as ice on the bay
yet always a circling
a pick in leather mittens

the night long enough to require
a fresh start unless you are a bear
willing to let the world
slide by while you sleep and dream
the fullness and satisfaction
of the toothless days of summer

Drifting Snow on an Unmarked Field

the fox has left his lair
you don't know where he hunts

mice cower in holes
voles crouch in runs

walk the field with your eyes clear
your arms open

move with the slant of sun
beneath the midday moon
its bent back a ghost in the winter sky

become the ocean of snow
curl between spruce to crest in their lee
stretch your fingers into the field

swim belly down in a drift
be an otter through snow
inhale icy dust

let your boots be filled
before you turn homeward
but keep your ears keen

you are the hunter

Winter Woman

days tighten to nuggets of glass
the fire holds me snugly until my heart
can't breathe and I release myself
onto the expanse of lake
scrape at ice enclosing water
my skin taut across my cheeks

my fingers ache when I grip the pick
lift the weight of it to let it bury itself in ice
over and over I circle and chip eventually
flip over the five gallon pail and pause
sit on the perch and let my eyes circle
the shoreline of spruce

across seasons of ice a woman stands in summer
in her flimsy dress   bare legs and bug bites
three children run to her swinging pails
faces and hands already purple from berries
there is a canoe pulled into the reeds
a deer browses further down the shore

in the belly of the canoe is a basket filled
with cold pancakes and apples   she kneels
by the bushes   picks quickly as she can

beneath my leggings and wool sweater
I remember her   watch as she tastes snow

Swans for Jane

I dig through the heart of winter toward midsummer heat
carry memories like coals in a moss pouch

in the year's pause I dangle questions
bare feet over a pond teeming with fish

I dream of limbs stretched against sand
the grit on my skin rasping me smooth

what I carry forward is more than desire

fossilized scents between layered days
rise unexpectedly as the dead

their ghosts wafting in the dip of swans
as they settle on the bay

Neighbourhood

latticework separates front from back
joins house to house all down the block
some hang with sweet peas   a few with scarlet runner beans
but most support roses   pink multi-petalled roses that lean
always away from the wood   arc into open air and sun
stems loosely bound by bands of old stockings

the lath crisscross like paths from door to neighbour's door
days upon months of traffic through the gap in the caragana hedge
across the lawn and up the step to the latest news
the newest disappointment   cup of coffee to sip
while the postal worker passes and the schoolyard across the street
blooms with children through recess

youngsters run between screen doors slamming
huddle under our maple picking seedwings
under Johnson's apple to eat windfalls
someone's mother calls us for cookies
another watches when a strange car slows
meatloaf and pie arrive at a house suddenly
busy with death

we huddle on the front walk with chalk and pebbles
pitch stones to the square we must not touch
carry that talisman in our pocket to the next opportunity
always waiting for the chance to leap one-legged
to the chalky moon   turn and hop home safe

Bowls (a set of five)

below a birch bluff harebells nod
between grass and goldenrod
a ridge of pebbles splays the curve
broken by a buffalo stone
crunchy with lichen

a bowl of earth
one small serving

~

robins ride spruce boughs as spring
winds rock their cradles   shreds of cloth
and leaves tangled with mud

the redpoll draws hazelnut whips together
lashes them tight with stems of grass
twists a cup of plantlets and moss

hollows of home woven to hold
skin and bone   eyes and beak

~

the pocket of my hand
lifts water to my lips
protects gifts
of butterfly wings

it's the curve that forms
snowballs
bread dough
hugs around cheeks

~

here in the cupboard there's one for cereal
another for fruit
the one Laurie's mom made kept in the freezer
its smooth sides ever ready
for whipped cream
rich garnish for pumpkin pie

while all the riches my children want
rest in a small bowl on the second shelf
coins to be rolled from time to time
divided into books and toy cars

children run indoors and out
collect treasure from bedroom and beach
pockets so full of stones
their pants slide to their knees
a button   a nickel   the knob
from the cabinet drawer
small and finely shaped
as the curve from forehead to nose

these bowls are filled with cookies and dirt
and not so funny knock-knock jokes
they feed on the scraps we toss
yet trail crumbs of innocent gold

Cave Painting

you stir my heart with simple
strokes and vital colors

my fingers want to trace
the outlines you have left

against the solidity of stone
I almost see the bison move

you scratch a line
draw blood

I force stones together until spark
sings its lullaby of light
wind breathes between rocks
weaves the stone circle

when I enter the cave
I come with fire in my veins
the red of horses runs with me
black bison threatens with his lowered head
but even the mammoth will feed me
if I am willing to ride it out of the night

flames singe my fingers
where rock draws blood
it flares into horses

pigment puddles like blood in a hollow
while stone holds the tool and the tale
today is an ochre bison
its hump and broken horn
remind us of life lost
ceremony raises a hand to bruise this surface
the cave curves around as we gather
fire leaps at my back
ochre preserves more than flesh

there is light on the steppes
and I would tell it
painted symbols the best
process I have to leave
notes to my children
for smoke drifts and arms grow tired
speakers are lost to beast or stone
so I paint on rock that does not wander
this cave both story and desire

in my careless awe I disturb
sanctuary and celebration
gawk at images once drawn to honor
beasts that granted tools and food

I rise with smoke from your blaze yet
would believe the blood of my fingers
is more complex

I carry a simple brush
in my left hand

Bones in the Street

raven
frog cousin
your watery croak
sounds spring in late October

I drink your sky
cold fills my lungs
I breathe out
and essence plumes the air

leaves of blood
burnt
bleached
are bones in the street
no one else sees skeletons
on the lawns of brick houses

a pot of daisies rises on the veranda
one small sun reluctant to let summer go
I'm wearing sandals while the woman
at the corner wears a parka

the rain falls
relentless

Crew Members Lost

did they look back as rain lashed and waves
surged between them and the failing ship
did the crew struggle to find direction or was it a resigned flow

she slumps in her chair
the child is sick again   rent is due
the principal is on the phone one more time wondering
what to do about her oldest and she answers
just do what you see fit
for there is no one else to hold the rudder

this is a ride in a boat she didn't build
her lines snarled before she made it any distance
her efforts unseen on the greater ocean

did those crew members toss up their hands
and rely on someone else to keep them safe
or were they striving every moment on their craft
to reach land   stay in sight of the wreck
every second an effort

neither trade route nor cruise line open to her
yet she kicks   tows the children with her
she struggles to keep her head up in this world

if the broken plank she clings to is snatched away
and the water reaches her chin
who will hold the line

the crew drifts
lost on the empty ocean

Raccoons and Multinationals

my neighbour's corn is disappearing
ear by ear into the night

listen   there is a rustling
that is not the wind

across the highway the sky is empty
there is no forest for lack of trees

the lake foams green yellow gray at the shore
the pelicans have not nested the past three years

every day more prints in the mud tell the tale
so much grief around the kitchen table where
coffee cups are refilled while words swirl
and traps attempt to snare the varmints

my neighbour never used to worry
about things going missing
now he's checking his shed
wondering what else slips away
under cover of night

Too Bad about the Devastation

it's a pity Hank ever built there
a single room cabin stretched to enfold
Jenna's rambling spirit

Jenna loved horses
too bad Hank idolized Jenna
let her heart's desire walk all over his head's sense

he hired some operator
willing to work nights for a couple of cases of beer
had him clear a training ring and space for a couple of corrals
but that wasn't enough room for Jenna and Hank

they spat and clawed their way out of the cozy all-loving cabin
until they stood at opposite corners of the new house
no one crossing the floor wide enough to dance on

Jenna lifted the bridle from the peg by the door
Hank threw the saddle after her   cinched it himself
stood in the driveway throwing words at trees

later the leaves grew every which way
the grass twisted all funny at the edge of the road
but whether that was from Hank's words
or Jenna's leaving
or the slashed hole in the forest
no one knew for sure

Meal Ticket for a Planet

spruce flash sunlight across the windshield
a truck passes with the roar of a hummingbird held in a tin can
my car leans stubbornly toward the ditch
the planet skews

I slow to a halt and climb out to stand on the verge
walk pensively around the vehicle then stand
by the bedraggled fence at the edge of the field
stare at the flat tire

my fingers are small sticks
my back a plank of reluctance
how easy it would be to call CAA
they seem willing to shoulder the responsibility
    a car is strangely bigger than itself
    with the ongoing need of fuel and oil and
    the endless scrape of rubber from tires

unexpected repairs tempt me to abandon
this outdated model for something newer
there must be a way out of this predicament
surely someone else can deal with it

but I hear my mother
her voice flows down the stairs from the kitchen
past the boys' bedrooms to the basement
where walls covered by old barn boards corral our noise
there's a Ouija board and a scatter of records on the floor
her words slip between the dog and the Monopoly money
clean up your mess
and I know I have to try
if I want any supper

Homegrown Magic

in the middle of town sleeps a garden
tended by a man who keeps the sun in his pocket
when the ice gets thin he pulls out light like a coin from an ear
watches trees waken   each one a hope for spring
every bud a bean in a cloth sack hanging from a rafter
egg cartons on windowsills bear a cargo of dirt and seeds
his root cellar hangs with patient bulbs in mesh bags
while a handful of potatoes huddle in a corner
each eye rooting for longer days

he balances the luxury of consumption
with the prudence of setting aside and allows
unused leaves and peelings to revisit the garden
he grants parsnips and carrots a second season
so delicate umbels of seed can contribute to tomorrow
the final round of peas fatten on the vine and
brittle canoes ferry pearls into the future
he knows there is not endless summer and so
processes green bean July to feed fruitless January

we choose to believe summer can be pulled from a hat
buy into the sleight of hand at the grocery store
fetch fresh strawberries and corncobs through winter winds
haul them home in a plastic bag past his sleeping
garden and the tiny house where jars
glow on their shelves with the intensity
of a midsummer rainbow

O

I.

seeds are in the ground and thirsty
so many mouths looking for a drink
in a dry land

round peas and radish
bean stretched to a smile
and O the carrot
dry and sharp
melon with its black tears
O the generous pumpkin

II.

the rabbit hole I escape through
O the carefree joy of dressing up
to become the unexpected
the mountain   the pearl
an accretion of character based on
inner agitation

the well I drink from
elongated O
the unblinking eye
of a day's reflection
pulled up in a dented pail

the bolt head O the nail head
that holds it all together

III.

O the goose egg
the nest
the nothingness of not being born
all that potential for being
ignored

IV.

my heart is the empty O
while you dwindle to
a speck in the distance
O the choking sounds from the closed throat
the noose that holds the careless foot
O the ring around the sun indicating a
change in weather
halo of darkness to come
winter in my mind

O is the gap
the chasm where we all become
void

I avoid you
fear reprisal in your eyes
know I haven't what you want

V.

burr the O that grips my sock
seed that clings because it wants to leave
this barren field
O

not big enough

Evening Medley in Moose Jaw

when light slides down the wall to shatter on the battered upright
the keys pick up the pieces   send quaver notes into evening
Stadacona Street East lifts itself out of the gloom
to swing on the scent of onions and apple pie

dwindling rays glide in arms of elms overhead
before they trip down shingles
cascade into sonorous green

children flicker between houses
their calls shrill contrast to the creeping
crescendo of purple that swells from eaves to hang in yards
echoes between cars parked at the curb

as the olive green of a sweater sways into dark
and night curls into the dangle of moon
the aches and squabbles of the day diminish
and all revive in the hum that augments tomorrow

No Way Back

Dean and I arrowed down alleys
corralled wild horses in the school yard
we flew trails as eagles hunting gophers in grass
ate peanut butter bread in the maple by the park
were daring enough to ride past approved limits
but were stunned when we didn't recognize houses
couldn't find the corner store and became
cautious until swift as curiosity
we set off again to discover the world

until Dean met the tailgate of a parked truck
our dash for the cup brought to a halt

I stood on the sidewalk while
adults rushed and Dean cried
his white face behind a car window
zooming away
Dean's bike remained on the lady's lawn
while I walked my own five blocks home

days passed
I hovered on his steps
not knowing what to do
with his broken arm and bruises
his mother repeatedly inviting me in
offering lemonade like medicine

slowly
this mishap
set us so far apart
we never found our way back

A Brief Note after Saying Goodbye

the phone rings and your voice in my ear
draws me out to meet you somewhere
over north Ontario   our words dangle
like legs over water   trip between
jumbled rocks on isolated shores
our murmurs fill the absence
good wishes smell
faintly of oranges

oranges
the fruit of separation
one that splits and splits
into complete tidy packages
tiny slivers within a sheath
all sweetness and zest
something to carry
away or leave behind
remembrance beneath our nails

this orange is for you
slim capsules of flesh packed
between white membranes
sliced with a knife
through dimpled skin
pierced to tears

my hand reaches to the bowl on my counter
as you say goodbye again
and again I am peeling
I lick my fingers
savouring the sting

Looking

I spent the entire day walking poplar brush and spruce groves
stretched out in waist-high grass in the meadow
                                                            beyond the birches
worked my slow way beneath the willows
                                                    where beaver wore a path
through stones that rim the slough next to Little Winter Lake
and when I doubled back
I ran into myself still coming out and saw
those impatient hands and scattered eyes
        eyes that flit like birds in search of food
        hoping here or there is sustenance
                hands that wander like coyotes across a field
                nosing potential hillocks yet rambling on dissatisfied

and I know it's been too long since I've been in the bush
I am stumbling and there's a red welt
across my nose where an alder whip sprang

usually the sweep of tamarack on my shoulder
slows me and I begin to unwind
but today I am a cocoon of worry
not ready to morph into peace
so I walk
looking outward
avoiding myself

Means of Navigation

she pauses on a bench drenched with autumn gold
considers the pale stems of birch heaped round with yellowed leaves
dark lenticels against bright bark are dashes of ducks overhead
their urge a mere blood-pulse in the thunder of summer

she envies those who wing unerringly home
they fly on faith while she struggles with possibilities
flips pages in her mind to scan for the exact
word that will give her that kind of insight

there is no cover binding the volume of geese traversing the sky
they have no trail to follow yet vee overhead with confidence
while she follows a path to the library almost obliterated by ivy
that knows it is time to turn colour

she wanders the stacks the way tracks criss-cross
mud at the edge of a hidden lake
pursues a map no one else can devise
her journey confined to the means she knows
    read every page
    memorize each line

Cloud Watching

I lay in the park the backs of my knees tickled by grass
watched a lazy whale stir swathes of white in the shifting sky

as a child I swam with my mouth gaped
wide like that of the right whale
great maw thrown open to take in gallons of seawater
sieve it out between close rows of baleen
retain copepod and krill to fill a huge belly
tiny tiny creatures to satisfy a great want

the sky has turned and the creature that once provided
meat and blubber in ideal proportion is almost extinct
its feeding range overwhelmed by whalers

and I no longer lie in grass to watch the upper ocean pass

I spend my time attempting to fulfill
expectations I never knew I had
restrict my diet until options
decline like whales and
caution limits me

the whale I might have been
lies in shallows
huge fins feeble

the sky has turned
I suffer hunger pangs every night

A Pocket of Humming

light splinters spruce bough and reeds
a bell tolls beyond the trees

ducks query across water
a small bridge gaps the chasm

sun trickles across grass   leaks
from the sandbox like summer's end

stones moan for the unnamed
foundations break and breathe

you sit in a pocket of humming
the end of your rope the fray of my hands

Not To Be Taken Lightly

(a reflection on the tar sands)

tenacious raven rides the back of a greasy half-ton
bears the past in his razored claws while he surveys the future
doesn't flinch from opportunity

fearless raven tears open bag after bag looking for treats
appreciates a meal easier come by
than what he might pick from a crack with a stick

gregarious raven loves to congregate where the world changes
sets up housekeeping in someone else's living room
even if it means his host is evicted

carefree raven rides downhill with wings spread
catches the wind in his coverts   no need to spin
his legs with the speed of wheels

adaptable raven back pedals across sky   wings cocked
feathers rumpled as he tumbles   safe in the hood
of his prehistoric head

Elusive Indications

doing dishes this morning I glimpsed a rabbit out the window
quivering ears with a glint of eye and a nose stretched above snow
then I lost her between a plate and a pot

just like comments we make in the Ford on the way to town
with the wind whining in past worn weather stripping
the radio distracting from the business at hand
those conversations at least one of us doesn't want to have
so it's best they take place
when the road needs watching
or there is an eagle over Dunn's field

I'm willing to focus on the vital spots
realize sometimes it's up to me
to stretch a little   meet you halfway
know there's something substantial in all those words yet wish
the inklings of what you mean wouldn't shift into shadow
the intent of your words becoming bits of fur
an ear lost in snow

Restoration

September sun piles ingots on my back
leaves rain from trees
pull the canopy
down
pool brilliance on the turning earth
naked branches brace the sky

grass weaves tarnished threads
as wind roams with a gentle heart
all is liquid amber

we are flies
our buzzing absent
from this brief window
our actions muted by the gargantuan day

even the snarl of saw slicing
a tree from itself
cannot open this day

Lunar Eclipse — Saskatchewan

mackerel swim a darkening sky and an owl
plunges in the fangs of a ravenous wind
tiny footprints dissolve in the snow`s shift

at the edge of a road hemmed by dark and bright
vapour rings my head and I stand safe
in the lonely hug of ski pants and parka

I know dark is not a devouring dragon
yet feel this rush of time
the strength of waves

the pause in a breath between draw and exhalation
is starlight on snow as the pendulum swings

a rind of moon cradles itself

Searching for Clues

a frenzy of tracks twists through willows
leads to the obvious tale of wait and pounce with its
iced over snow   fur   blood melt
there is more in this scene that eludes me

        the patience
to crouch and linger beneath a spruce bough
when the air is minus forty and the forest is motionless
to trust that a rabbit will happen by
to be that quick after hours of immobility
and then to abandon the prize
one hind quarter
on the shoulder of a gravel road

the raven knows
and arrives
to abscond with the haunch

the human
comes back again
and again
searching for clues

Snowbound

a void waits to be filled

snow tucks a blanket
snug to the feet of naked aspen

I dream a fence that limits a field

a sliver of rail drills into my palm
it pivots east   point of beginnings

I am hungry
kindle a fire that waits for a pan
a blaze that burns blue
the sign of excellent moonshine
the sign that says there will be
no ill effects

still my breath comes slow
not enough oxygen
like the blue baby whose heart
is not perfect   none of us are

we love as best we can
live with inadequacy

lintels slide from doorways
these stones will not be lifted

in the morning there will be footprints

No Stopping Us

we rose with a gleam restless as bicycle wheels
spun down the road to the local amusement park
woke the sleeping giant with punches in his belly
our feet pushed into taut canvas bouncing us skyward
where we twisted contortions in the warming air

we blazed through playgrounds
pulled ourselves hand over hand from platform to slide
swung wide over the farthest sand to dare the monster
felt the graze of his claws on ankles
the trace of his touch up our spines

but we simply pulled harder   ran faster
wind the breath that pushed the leaves
the secret ingredient that made the magic
potion we stirred and stirred
to brew invisibility   strength

we caught one another jumping from roofs
when wings wouldn't sprout
crawled out of windows and
teetered on fences
there was no looking back

we prowled beneath the footbridge
seeking bugs and the longest worm
not noticing the passage of time
moon rising
slicing the sky into before and after

Rope of Days

I am twisting this rope of days
harsh in my hands
                    pulling in
      early mornings to beat the sun
      long hours of walking and carrying loads
      coffee breaks that end prematurely
                    winding in
      a strand of slow mornings
      on the deck with chickadees and squirrels
      lazier evenings with feet to the fire
      an ear to the coyotes
                    coiling in
      a filament of talk
      late night discussion with heads against pillows
      words into the dark like moths searching for light
      bunting themselves useless against the screen

all my effort without results
muscles aching and hands
so tired they can't hold a coffee cup
can't pull start the mower

too tired to think
too stupid to stop
the effort of wanting
the want of no effort
no time no time no time

I’m twisting these days in my hands
a long rope that I hope
is strong enough to pull me out
less likely to snap
than that rigging of chains that slingshot
into the windshield of the truck
every link impressed
in the crazed glass

Galls

yours socks still lay at the foot of the bed
like lint on a rug or twine in grass
waiting for some fervent robin to weave
into a sturdy nest along with the rest
of the clay you've been slinging

these bits are not what makes a cozy home
they are more like sand in shoes than particles in oysters
they will not create pearls

galls
all those unasked for comments
every time you assume what I am going to say
when I barely know myself

willows form galls when a bug gets into a flower bud
seals itself in and reproduces in hope
of surviving harsh conditions
comes out in spring to do it again
eventually destroying its host

Not Listening

I'm too busy inside my head hearing words spin off the sun like water droplets off a whirling toy that's been dipped in the lake. They fly out to strike the sand, the chair, the dryness of a yellow shirt. Those fat splotches arrest my attention, and it's not that I don't want to hear about your lousy day but when you say frustrating my mind elves jump up and build fences and I'm painting them purple and blue, laying the groundwork for a short, curving path to a bench by the sea. Then my errant ear catches another phrase so I lean into the pause and I'm back — stepping into a void risky as any bear trap, a misplaced comment, the opportunity to lose a leg. Who can blame you for your rolled eyes and *here we go again* look. My jelly self resolves to stay focussed, but the ear turns loosely, searching for a signal that resonates: word or cadence, shift of light, almost anything will do.

This Hunger

from the still of the room she hears the train
its insistence tugs her to the window
grants no satisfaction
all she craves is the sway of boxcars
run and swing aboard   ride them hobo style
take her empty self to some central terminal that divulges
purpose in a chute separate from chaff
blown into wide open space

she has conversations over the phone
        the weather has turned and its almost
        too cold to go for a load of wood
                that overdue paper won't finish itself
                but the band at the club was hot hot hot
all volume and tone
she hangs on the words the way socks on the line fill
with wind then collapse when tossed into a drawer

there's a thrum in the night that calls
to the space in her heart
enough to pull her out of bed
she nibbles apples   then almonds
seeks the right combination
this hunger so subtle
the way it sidles up to bitter

All My Rivers Run from Here

it cannot be one continuous climb through brambles
while the stove ticks in the background and the fridge hums
my boots dry by the door

the sink fills slowly like my mind in the morning
dawn washes the sky
I do not want to be stuck
at an endless counter of dishes
so I toss them
hear their chatter on stones
they cry in broken voices
and I turn away

opportunity stands in the doorway with her big boots
she holds a paddle to serve up the world   knocks
only once (maybe twice)
people learn soon enough there is no
coffee in the cup   no pot on the stove

I slide my feet into boots and wander
not just the trail through the pasture
nor the one by the lake but roam
until I am lost in a field encircled by forest

I slip into sandals and climb
into the car with my shoulder bag
and two friends and pitch
the map to the wind

I bring home the peace of solitude
and the antics of a road trip
so I can lean into the sweet evening fiddle
share moments around a flickering blaze

Steel Spins On

I dream of riding a red train past poplar and birch
winding into towns and out of worry
my jerky sway subject only to the brown-eyed
gaze of indifferent cows
I wish I was purchasing a ticket

if only my days would link together
defy the shunt of cars onto sidings
that slow squeal coupled with the long push
I want tracks that stretch out like a cat in the morning
spun steel and possibility

I once walked along tracks with sun on my head
welcomed the trickle of sweat down my back
while miles piled up like stones beneath ties
ticking my feet like a stick on a fence until my thoughts
fell like pennies on tracks

when I smell wild sage and tar
I think of rails through prairie
slicing it open
letting out the deep earth smell
the gash in an orange that releases its essence
          and my fingers stick to themselves

someday I will leave the station
stretch my legs the way rails curve a rise
follow a filament of steel snaking grass

in the future my eyes will be blue
a blue this train can curl into
as it leaves the muddy station

Woman as Otter

beneath spruce boughs there's an ice nest
formed by a warm body lying for hours
in the protected hollow between earth and sky
sinuous troughs wind like spruce roots between trunks
to and fro brackets that mark
the struggle to gather things together

then there's all that's left out
foretracking   backtracking
the other side of the road where
a wandering mind in its restless search
erases all logic and landmarks
sprays living blood on snow

one day I wake up ravenous
unsure where this bloodletting will take me
but this time there is no stopping
my tracks a confusion
that return to this spot
frozen on the road

and it's not about hunger anymore
it's mostly about viciousness
wanting to make something bleed
I want you/it/them to feel my pain
my frustration
my no solution

Riding Double

After the moon is free of the trees, our shadows sharp as the air we breathe, we clear the yard in a flurry of horse hooves and snow. I hope for something more than kindling in the woodbox, more than oats in the trough. I'm ready to let myself go into the dark, enter the void lit by distant stars where I have no answers. Riding up to the ridge, our laughter carries in the calm air, moonlight on snow plays tricks with our eyes.

But as we ready to leave the neighbour's a friend wants to join us, a friend without a horse. How can I not agree to ride double; how could I not be willing to share? My adventure retreats, moon behind clouds, my need for just me slinks away. Resentment, small weasel, slips into my pocket, in spite of the warmth, in spite of the laughter and jostling. We ride across Winter Lake, spooking three deer bedded beneath spruce at the shore.

Over the meadow I fling my arms wide, stretch for all that slips away. Suddenly none of it matters. It's not important who holds the reins; I don't care who has to get up with the kids in the morning.

I am an owl slow-flying over the midnight field clutching the moment in my greedy talons. I lift it kicking from snow, haul it home to my nest, high in an aspen at the edge of the ravine, far beyond the power line.

December: a meditation

the first flakes of winter
drift by the window
remind me of seasons
lost to summer suns

slow days with no fields to turn
sharp breath in the iron air
I carry a load in my arms
set it down only to sleep

my blood crawls
cold stones lie content
in the wide river

banks twist through the earth
grass mats cushioned with snow
are prayer rugs for my knees

I am caught in the arms of spruce
suspended as ice over water

a twig fire burns
the quick snap of flame
singes my careless glove

my eyes lock at the snowline
don't see robins on grass
geese overhead

I cower with spruce grouse
inert   hiding
silent wings beating
lessons into bone

While We Wait

hang your head out the window of a beat up Ford
let the world view your rear molars as you jaw-drop
and your tongue lolls out the corner of your mouth
the same way I hang off the couch on mid-winter Saturdays
everything frozen to its core and thawed prematurely
bloody roast drips from the kitchen counter

there is no passion in reports that cross your desk
all energy expended in keeping the car
moving down the snowy lane
there is no verve in discussions after exercise class
even stretches fall flat and shadows of myself
refuse to writhe on the gymnasium floor

you are one of the jaunty
who lean hardest against winter
with its demand for pause and reflection
while I dream the pink blooms of bergenia
admire its ability to lie flaccid in frost and
survive to stand erect the next season

we wait
for a day when the sun catches the cold
that has burdened you with resolve and good cheer
and allows you to relax in mid-March leniency

we wait for spring
when the snow slumps itself off the deck and I can roam
outside in sweat pants with my hair a mess but no one notices
since the blue squill is making
sky puddles in the mire of last fall's leaves
and the neighbours tulips are bleeding against the house

Ties That Bind

it wasn't the Sunday suppers or Christmases with cousins
or the all-day picnics at Buffalo Pound that kept us together
it was the trips to the bakery on Main Street

Nana pulled open the door too heavy for me
and the sweet yeasty smell gusted out to envelope us
we waited our turn while racks of bread loomed
in the dim passage to the rear   their round humps glistening
at the front of the store cakes with ripples and roses of icing
leaned toward the glass
and cookies lay in long rows

always the bread first
practicality before delight
but I waited for the cookies and the making of the box
a sheet of white cardboard bent and tucked into a neat shape
then the clerk lifting Nana's requests
gingersnap   sugar   oatmeal raisin   chocolate chip
one pleasure after another sliding into the square nest

the clerk snared the tail of string that curled on the counter
tugged a length from the huge spool above my head
and wrapping it around and over
crossed it neatly without ever tipping the box
tied a snug knot and taking a twist around her hand
broke the string
freeing the box to follow me out the door

in my hand a gift
small doily gritty with sweetness
I nibbled the cookie's edge trying to duplicate the tiny scallops
soon enough my treat was licked fingers
and sugar in the corner of my mouth

at home Nana   with careful hands
set the white box on the small table

removed her coat then placed her hat
high on the shelf in the front hall
she carried the cookie box to the kitchen counter
opened the drawer and removed the paring knife
the blade so thin it whispered
she cut the string right at the knot so
the length of it was all it could be
added it to the string ball that rested
on the corner shelf

I imagined taking that string sphere outside
tying the loose end to the door latch
and tossing the globe in the air
string looping between the handrail flaky with paint
and the clothesline pole holding up one end of the sky
I dreamt of letting the fine twine trail
between peonies safe in their wire cages
of running a strand from the garage door
back to the rose trellis
all diamonds and thorns

but I was afraid the unravelling
might be more than string
sensed somehow this collecting
was more important than I knew
had to do with the careful keeping
of things brought home in bits
and with diligence
bound together

How Does the Sun Go

she travels the kitchen a spoon in her hand
lifts boxes of produce from the porch to a chair
        years ago her bubba chopped cabbage
        pressed it into a heavy crock
        to hold all that goodness down
        with a plate and a clean stone
        waited for it to change

tomato juice patterns the floor like
rosettes of beads decorate moccasins
        she has never sliced a haunch yielded
        from the bison   jerked it to dryness
        but she'd like to pound berries
        would split fish to hang from racks
        that stand in the summer sun

restless   she turns stove to door
enters the forest   oasis from vinegar
and mustard seed   beyond cultivation
cleared of tomato vines   she moves
into the bush of childhood where
she knew the berries and trusted the fungi

her tired fingers seek spruce bark the way
a child gropes for the hip of her mother

Lessons

between the leaves of Labrador tea hang the warm
afternoons the children spent leaping from rock to
rock in the shallow waters off the point

the white spruce lean into the land
the way the children tend toward home
when the bite of the world threatens to bleed
they know about leeches between toes and they
all bear the scars of slipping from stones

they remember how it was to run
for the salt shaker tucked in the hollow
at the base of the pitched spruce and wait
and wait while the leech squirmed and finally
fell onto sand or
when a wave caught them unexpectedly
and the lake burned in the back of their noses
until they squeezed the water out slowly   without panic
and breathed again

I think about leeches I have let cling
like the woman who calls for coffee demanding
attention but not hearing my voice
it's time to shake them loose
let them fall with the rest of the grit I sweep from my floor
I recall the sting in the back of my nose from tears never shed
and know it's time to breathe again

the trick is knowing where the rocks are
remembering to put my feet down

Palimpsest

some marks stay
like the blue crayon Sam scribbled on the kitchen wall
while the rest of us sipped coffee on the deck

even though we scrubbed and diligently repainted
each cursive shadows the next and next

a story set in lemon juice waits for a lamp to reveal the truth
but the cipher and its solution are lost in the wash
no mordant is powerful enough to fossilize everything
while memory shifts like cloth in an alum bath
and not even time is strong enough
to bleach it out like bones adrift in unfenced pastures

we accumulate like the walls in my sister's new old house
layered with paint then paper until finally more paint attempts to
deny years' accretions of personal preference and designer styles
        faded squares hang on the walls like pictures
        a halo of grease hovers about the stove

it's the punctuation of nail holes
those small openings
that allow the slow adding on
as what was
becomes
impeccably itself

Word Children

slams and jackets and words
tumble in the door
the toys are out
and cars zip across linoleum
a puzzle jumbles with crayons

the big bowl rests on the counter surrounded by words
who will stir   *who will crack the eggs*
I draw my fingers through small spills
bring them to my tongue

words lean into my hip   place stones
in my palm *see the sparkle?*
I bend to see the tiniest bug
but it's *too late — gone into a hole*

we rubber boot ramble
in the patter of rain on poplar leaves
come in to a quick supper
until I send the words running
falling over themselves to be
the first one in the tub
the first on the couch for a story
I stand aside to watch the mad dash

and I welcome these words
wash my hair to their rain
this brief shower
a downpour that washes the gutter

The Rock

In the middle of the yard, at the top of the slope, squats a huge rock. Children climb it to prove they aren't little anymore. The rest of us sit on the deck, that no man's land between house and yard, and watch. Four kids between five and eleven tumble up and down the rock the way squirrels go up and down a spruce tree. Three three-year-olds ring the rock, their arms stretched up as far as they can reach. Someone begins to build a fire in the pit, a circle of stones waiting for a warm heart to drive out the soggy remains. Slowly we drift down to the grass, into the chairs and onto the benches. An armload of wood is collected from the stack below the house and left handy next to a stump. Someone begins skinning out the moose, nails those antlers, the wings of some huge bird, to the spruce tree. Potatoes, lumps of fuel to feed human fires, are poked into the flames. A patient woman turns and turns those lumps, drags out a chunk, mashes and blows on it and offers it to the baby. A tray bearing plates and forks joins the jug of water on the weather-worn table. The dogs skulk at the edge of the yard, half crazy with the smell of fresh meat, but they know not to be underfoot or begging except for Bran, old dog who won't quit, who gets locked in the porch where he barks and whines. And whoever isn't picking up a fallen child or roasting moose strips on a carefully rigged rack over glowing coals, slides into the house and out again with a guitar or fiddle. Evening fades and tones change as even the dogs are fed. The fiddle sings the children down from the rock to lean on legs and climb into the laps resting around the fire.

We’re the Big Kids Now

it’s best when we go bike riding to escape boredom and heat
the paddling pool close but too shallow for satisfaction
eleven too old to be puddling around up to our knees in toddlers
spray pours over the bow of our speed boat chasing robbers and
mothers give us the evil eye when the waves get high
that two year old is screaming
her face is wet and we all know it’s time to leave

we leap
ocean to air
flying in the fastest jet
cruising at altitude over the park

we fly from meeting to conference
rush in the door when we finally reach home
only to pick up the phone   flick on a computer
we forget to play
think we’re the king of the mountain

looking down on all the tiny people
even the adults look like ants

Scratching on Stubble

we are geese drawn to sun-hot summerfallow
we swirl
outline an arc beyond the aspen bluff
rise over the trio of granaries
until we are drawn to the field
open space where we have room
to flap our wings   arch necks
we flourish and circle   come around

again and again the same argument
a fresh slant with alternate words
the sun going down bruises the clouds

some geese have beaks tucked
beneath a wing
others feed on spilled grain

is it a matter of being convinced
or is it simply being
too tired to argue anymore?

one final pass
the weight of words sinking
in the cooling air
as willows concede to evening

the approach to earth with tail down
wings extended until
feet scratch stubble
and we fold as the air stills

Song

down an overgrown track beyond the willows
I glimpse the burned-out husk of a '65 Ford
remnants of the time some high school kids
partied through the night until
someone smoking in the coupe's back seat
passed out and was rescued
when his friends saw the smoke

today all that remain
are bread crusts the squirrels haven't found yet
and a child's sandal beside a flattened square of grass
near the lake where a blanket corralled a family
and their picnic

I can almost hear the music that fell
from the windows of the car
and the mother's voice chanting with her children
the words to their games

the sun on my arms is warm as the blaze
of the campfire that once burned on this spot
where voices overwhelmed guitar and mandolin

wind whistles across the tops of bottles
plugged in mud at the shore
by drinkers of pop or milk or beer

glass mouths that give
and take the wind
to form words

all our lives
being sung